# RASPBERRY PI

## Step-by-Step Guide To Mastering Raspberry PI 3 Hardware and Software

## Richard Ray

# TABLE OF CONTENTS

CHAPTER 1 ................................................. 5

INTRODUCTION TO RASPBERRY PI ............................. 5

CHAPTER 2 ................................................. 14

GETTING STARTED WITH THE RASPBERRY PI ............. 14

CHAPTER 3 ................................................. 24

INTRODUCTION TO EMBEDDED LINUX ...................... 24

CHAPTER 4 ................................................. 33

WORKING WITH ELECTRONICS ................................. 33

CHAPTER 5 ................................................. 41

PROGRAMMING A RASPBERRY PI ............................ 41

CHAPTER 6 ................................................. 55

INPUT AND OUTPUT ON A RASPBERRY PI .................. 55

CHAPTER 7 ................................................. 73

**INTRODUCTION TO COMMUNICATION PROTOCOLS .. 73**

**CHAPTER 8** .................................................................. 92

**PYTHON PROGRAMMING FOR THE RASPBERRY PI..... 92**

**CHAPTER 9** ................................................................. 123

**FINAL PROJECT** ........................................................ 123

# Chapter 1

# Introduction to Raspberry Pi

**What you will learn in this chapter:**

📔Raspberry Pi boards

📔Raspberry Pi hardware

**What you will need for this chapter:**

📔Raspberry Pi board

The Raspberry Pi was developed to encourage children who want to learn about computers and programming. The Raspberry Pi is one of the most popular devices in the system-on-a-chip (SoC) market, thanks to its rapid development and the low cost, which starts from just $5 for the Raspberry Pi Zero model. In 2015, more than five million

Raspberry Pi boards were sold. The Raspberry Pi boards are very complex, but the ability of the Raspberry Pi to run embedded Linux makes the device both powerful and accessible. Using Linux on embedded systems makes the development very easy, especially if we develop applications for smart things, the Internet of Things (IoT), robotics, smart cities, and cyber-physical systems. Thanks to the integration between Linux software and electronics, this board represents a paradigm shift in the development of embedded systems. You can use the Raspberry Pi not only in embedded systems development but also as a general purpose computer.

As we said before, the Raspberry PI can be used as a general purpose computing device. Because of that reason, it may be used to introduce computer programming to its users, but most of the developers use it as an embedded Linux platform.

Most of the Raspberry Pi models have the following features:

- Low cost, starting from $5 to $35

- Contains a powerful 1.2 GHz ARM Cortex – A53 processor which can process more than 700 million instructions per second

- Has many models that are suitable for different applications

- They save a lot of power since they run at 0.5W to 5.5W

- If you need support for any project, you can easily find a solution thanks to the huge community of innovators

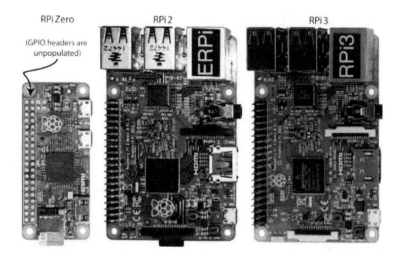

- It can run a Linux operating system, so you can install open source libraries and many applications directly to it

It has Hardware Attached on Top (HATs)

This actually an impressive feature because you can extend the Raspberry Pi functionality using HAT that then connects to the GPIO header, so you can design your own HATs and attach them to your Raspberry Pi header.

If you want to learn about electronics, programming, and the Linux operating system, you should use the Raspberry Pi platform especially for IoT applications and robotics.

The Raspberry PI is better than other embedded Linux devices and more traditional embedded systems, such as the Arduino, AVR, and PIC microcontrollers, is when you use Linux for your project. For example, if we develop a smart home system using the Raspberry Pi and you want to make information on the Internet, you can use and install the Nginx web server. After that, you can use a server-side language like PHP, Python, Perl, or any other programming language you may prefer. Also, you may want remote shell access, so you could install a Secure Shell without any effort by using the command: sudo apt install sshd. This will save you time.

On Linux operating systems you will find device driver support for many USB peripherals that makes the installation of any USB device so easy like camera, Wi-Fi adapters, and much more, instead of complex software drivers.

The Raspberry Pi can also play HD videos because it has a Broadcom BCM2835/6/7 processor used for multimedia applications, and it also a has a hardware implementation of H.264 MIPG-4 and MPG-2/VC-1 decoders and encoders.

If you are going to develop applications for a real time system then the Raspberry Pi will not be a good choice. For example, if you want to use a sensor to get some values every on millions of a second, it will be not easy to interrupt the system, but you can connect them with real-time micro-controllers through the buses like UART, 12C and Ethernet.

# Raspberry Pi Hardware

The heart of every Raspberry Pi board is the Broadcom BCM2835, BCM2836, and BCM2837 system-on-a-chip (SoC). Raspberry Pi models are available for example (the Raspberry Pi A+, B+, 2, 3 and Zero), but I recommend purchasing the Raspberry Pi 3 because it has a multi-core processor.

## Raspberry Pi Versions

● If you want to use the Raspberry Pi as a general purpose computer, you should consider the Raspberry Pi 3. The 1 GB of memory and 1.2 GHz processor provides the best performance compared to the other boards.

● For applications that interface electronics to the Internet on a network, use the Raspberry Pi 3 2 or Raspberry Pi B+.

● If you want a small board with wireless capability , the best choice would be the Raspberry Pi Zero

| Model | RPi 3 | RPi 2 | RPi B+ | RPi A+ | RPi Zero | RPi B | Compute |
|---|---|---|---|---|---|---|---|
| Characteristics | performance/Wi-Fi Bluetooth/Ethernet | performance/Ethernet | Ethernet | price | price/size | original | integration/eMMC |
| Price | $35 | $35 | $25 | $20 | $5+ | $25 | $40 ($30 volume) |
| Processor* | BCM2837 quad core Linux ARMv7 | BCM2836 quad core Linux ARMv7 | BCM2835 Linux ARMv6 | BCM2835 Linux ARMv6 | BCM2835 Linux ARMv6 | BCM2835 Linux ARMv6 | BCM2835 Linux ARMv6 |
| Speed | 1.2 GHz | 900 MHz | 700 MHz | 700 MHz | 1 GHz | 700 MHz | 700 MHz |
| Memory | 1GB | 1GB | 512 MB | 256 MB | 512 MB | 512 MB | 512 MB |
| Typical power | 2.5 W (up to 6.5 W) | 2.5 W (up to 4.1 W) | 1 W (up to 1.5 W) | 1 W (up to 1.5 W) | 1 W (up to 1.5 W) | 1 W (up to 1.5 W) | 1 W (up to 1.5 W) |
| USB Ports | 4 | 4 | 4 | 1 | 1 OTG | 2 | via header |
| Ethernet | 10/100 Mbps, Wi-Fi, and Bluetooth | 10/100 Mbps | 10/100 Mbps | none | none | 10/100 Mbps | none |
| Storage | micro-SD | micro-SD | micro-SD | micro-SD | micro-SD | SD | 4GB eMMC |
| Video | HDMI composite | HDMI composite | HDMI composite | HDMI composite | mini-HDMI composite | HDMI RCA video | HDMI via edge TV DAC via edge |
| Audio | HDMI digital audio and analog stereo via a 3.5mm jack (where available) | | | | | | via edge connector |
| GPU | Dual Core VideoCore IV Multimedia Co-Processor at 250 MHz (24 GFLOPS) | | | | | | |
| Camera (CSI) | yes | yes | yes | yes | no | yes | CSI x 2 via edge |
| Display (DSI) | yes | yes | yes | yes | no | yes | DSI x 2 via edge |
| GPIO header | 40 pins | 40 pins | 40 pins | 40 pins | 40 pins | 26 pins | 48 pins via edge |
| Usage | General-purpose computing and networking. High-performance interfacing. Video streaming | General-purpose computing. High-performance interfacing. Video streaming | General-purpose computing. Internet-connected host. Video streaming | Low-cost general-purpose computing. Standalone electronics interfacing applications | Low-cost small-profile standalone electronics interfacing projects | General-purpose applications. Internet-connected host | Suitable for plugging into user-created PCBs using a DDR2 SODIMM connector. Open-source breakout board available |

Details in this table were gleaned from articles and documents from the RPi Foundation website (www.raspberrypi.org).

* The BCM2835 is an ARM1176JZF-S (ARM11 processor architecture) that has full entitlement to an ARMv6 software architecture. The BCM2836 is a quad-core ARM Cortex-A7 processor that has a NEON Data Engine and full entitlement to an ARMv7 software architecture. The BCM2837 is a 64-bit ARMv8 quad-core ARM Cortex-A53 processor that has a NEON Data Engine and full entitlement to an ARMv7 software architecture.

Now let's take a closer look of the Raspberry hardware.

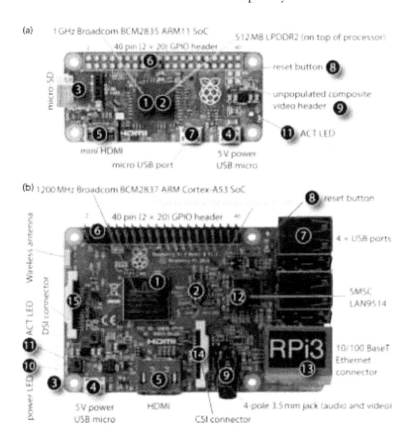

**1. Processor**: The Raspberry Pi uses the Broadcom BCM2835/BCM2836/BCM2837 processor.

**2. Memory:** The amount of system memory affects performance and the use of the Raspberry Pi as a general purpose computer. Memory is shared between the CPU and GPU (256 MB to 1GB DDR).

**3. Storage:** The Raspberry PI boards all boot from a micro SD or SD card, with the exception of the computer module. It has an on-board eMMC, which is effectively an SD card on a chip. The Raspberry PI 3 uses a friction-fit slot, rather than a click in/click out slot

**4. Power:** A 5v supply is required that can ideally deliver a current of at least 1.1A and 2.5A for the Raspberry Pi 3. Be careful not to continue the USB hub and USB power inputs on the Raspberry Pi Zero.

**5. Video Out:** Used to connect the Raspberry Pi boards to a monitor or television. The Raspberry Pi models support 14 output resolutions, including full-HD (1920 x 1080) and 1920 x 1200.

**6. GPIOs:** 40 pins that are multiplexed to provide access to the following features (2x I2C, SPI bus, UART, PWM, GPCLIK).

**7. USB:** There is an internal USB hub on Raspberry Pi models with varying numbers of inputs.

**8. Reset:** Can be used to reset the Raspberry Pi.

**9. Audio and video:** This provides composite video and stereo audio on the Raspberry PI.

**10. Power LED:** Indicates that the board is powered.

**11. Activity LED:** Indicates that there is activity on the board.

**12. USB to Ethernet:** This IC provides a USB 2.0 hub and a 10/100 Ethernet controller.

**13. Network:** 10/100 Mbps Ethernet via a RJ45 connector.

**14. Camera:** The Raspberry Pi has a mobile industry processor interface camera serial interface, a 15-pin connector that can be connected to a special purpose camera.

**15. Display:**  The Display Serial Interface is an interface that is typically used by mobile phone vendors to interface with a screen display.

# Questions for Chapter 1

1. What is the Raspberry Pi?

2. Describe the difference between the different Raspberry PI boards.

3. What are the HATs?

4. Describe the usage of the display on the Raspberry Pi.

5. Is the Raspberry Pi board good for real time system? Why or why not?

# Chapter 2

# Getting Started with the Raspberry Pi

**What you will learn in this chapter:**

📠 Understanding Linux

📠 Raspberry Pi software

**What you will need for this chapter:**

📠 Raspberry Pi board

USB cable

Micro-SD card

Serial cable or Wi-Fi adapter

Linux has many distributions (also known as versions) of its operating system. There are many different Linux versions such as Debian, Red Hat, or OpenSUSE that are mainly used on servers, but versions like Ubuntu, Fedora, or Linux Mint are used for desktop users. But you should keep in mind that they all have the same Linux kernel that was created by Linus Torvalds in 1991.

For an embedded system we will choose a distribution based on the following:

● The stability of the distribution

● The package manger

● The level of community support for the device used

● The device drivers support

**Linux for the Raspberry Pi**

As we said before that every Linux version has its own tools and configurations that result in a quite different user experience, the main open source Linux versions used on the Raspberry Pi board include Raspbian, Arch Linux, and Ubuntu.

Raspbian is a version of Debian; there are three versions of Raspbian on the Raspberry Pi website:

• **Raspbian Jessie:** An image based on Debian version 8.

• **Raspbian Jessie Lite:** A minimal image based on Debian Jessie, but with limited desktop support.

• **Raspbian Wheezy:** An older image based on Debian version 7.

• The Ubuntu distro (a distribution) is very close to Debian as described on the Ubuntu website "Debian is the rock upon which Ubuntu is built."

• Ubuntu is one of the most popular distributions because it has excellent desktop driver support, is easy to install, and is more accessible to new users.

• Arch Linux is a lightweight Linux version targeting competent Linux users. Prebuilt versions of the Arch Linux distribution are available for the Raspberry Pi, but it has less support for new Linux users that use the Raspberry Pi platform.

• The Raspberry Pi Foundation developed a Linux installer called NOOBS. It contains Raspbian but also provides the download and installation of other Linux distributions as well.

### Let's create a Linux SD card image for the Raspberry PI

• If you want to set up an SD card to boot the Raspberry Pi, just download a Linux distribution image file from www.raspberrypi.org/downloads and write it to an SD card using any image writer.

### Connect to a Network

There are two ways to connect the Raspberry Pi to a network using regular Ethernet or an Ethernet crossover cable.

| Advantages | Disadvantages |
|---|---|
| You will have control over IP address settings | You will need administrative control |
| You can connect many boards | You will need a source power for the Raspberry Pi over Ethernet |
| The Raspberry Pi can connect to the Internet without a desktop computer | The setup is more complex for beginners |

● The first thing you should do is find your Raspberry Pi on the network. By default, the Raspberry Pi request a Dynamic Host Configuration Protocol (DHCP) IP address. This service is provided by the DHCP server that runs on the integrated modem – router –LAN.

You can use any of the following methods to get the Raspberry Pi's dynamic IP address:

● Using a web browser: write 192.168.1.1, 192.168.0.1 or 10.0.0.1. Log in and look under the menu "Status" for the DHCP Table. You should see an entry with the details for the IP address, the MAC address, and the lease time remaining for a device with the hostname Raspberry Pi.

● Using a port scanning tool: Use a tool such as nmap under Linux or the Zenmap GUI version available for Windows. You will search for an entry has an open port 22 for SSH. It identifies the range of MAC addresses to the foundation. You can ping it to test the network connection.

## Let's use the other type which is the Ethernet crossover cable

An Ethernet crossover cable is a cable that has been modified to enable similar devices to connect without using a switch.

| Advantages | Disadvantages |
| --- | --- |
| In case you don't have access to the network , you can still connect the Raspberry Pi | When your desktop machine has only one network adapter, you will lose access to the Internet |
| Raspberry Pi can have Internet access if you have two network adapters and sharing is enabled | Raspberry Pi will need a source of power |
| You will have a stable network setup | You may need a specialized crossover cable |

**Here are the steps when you use the Windows operating system**

1. Plug one end of the cable into the Raspberry Pi and the other end into the laptop socket.

2. Turn on the Raspberry Pi by attaching the micro-USB power supply.

3. Open up the Control Panel, choose Network Connections, then select two network adapters (wired and wireless). At the same time, right click and choose bridge connection.

4. Restart the Raspberry Pi. You can use a USB or TTL serial cable to do this, or use the reset button directly, then your Raspberry Pi will get an IP address from the DHCP server.

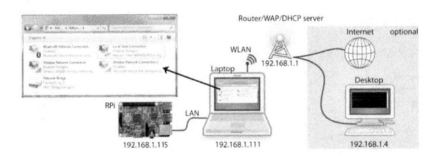

## Communicating with Raspberry Pi

After you networked the Raspberry PI, the next thing that you will need to do is communicate with the Raspberry Pi. You can connect the Raspberry Pi using a serial connecting over USB to TTL or using a network connection as we did before. It is a fallback communication method for when something goes wrong with the software services on the Raspberry Pi board. You can also use it to configure wireless networking on the Raspberry Pi.

To connect the Raspberry pi through the serial connection, you will need terminal software; you can choose PuTTY or RealTeerm on Windows. If you are using a Linux OS, press Ctrl + Alt+T then type gnome-terminal under Debian.

To find the port number, open the Windows Device Manager, and find where the device is. It is listed as COMx.

Set up the connection speed; by default it will be 115,200 baud to connect the Raspberry Pi.

Then set the following values: bits = 8; Stop bits=1; Parity=none; and Flow control = XON/.XOFF.

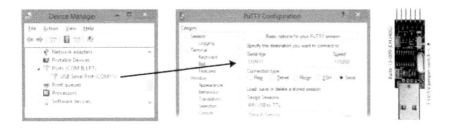

## Connecting the Raspberry PI via SSH

Secure Shell (SSH) is a useful network protocol for secure encrypted communication between network devices. The SSH is running on port 22, and you can also use Putty to connect the Raspberry PI via SSH.

**Basic Linux Commands**

| Command | Description |
|---------|-------------|
| More/etc/issue | Returns the Linux Version |
| pp –p $$ | Returns the shell you are suing (like bash) |
| whoami | Returns who you are logged in as |
| uptime | Returns how long the system has been running |
| top | Lists all of the processes and programs executing |
| | |

File system Commands

| Name | Command | Information | Example |
|------|---------|-------------|---------|

21

| | | | |
|---|---|---|---|
| **List files** | ls | Show all files | ls –alh |
| **Current directory** | pwd | Show the working directory | pwd -p |
| **Change directory** | cd | Change directory | cd / |
| **Make a directory** | mkdir | Create a directory | mkdir new |
| **Delete directory** | rm | Delete directory | rm new |
| **Copy a directory** | cp | Recursive copy | cp new new2 |
| **Create an empty file** | touch | Create an empty file | touch f.txt |
| **Get the calendar** | cal | Display the calendar | cal 7 2017 |

# Questions for Chapter 2

1.  Describe some of Linux's features.

2.  What is the SSH protocol?

3.  List the advantages and disadvantages for the crossover Ethernet cable.

4.  Which command you will use to show the current working directory?

# Chapter 3

# Introduction to Embedded Linux

**What you will learn in this chapter:**

Raspberry Pi boards

**What you will need for this chapter:**

Understanding Embedded Linux

More Linux commands

Intro to Git

First of all, the term embedded Linux is technically not one hundred percent correct because there is no special Linux kernel for embedded systems; it's the same Linux kernel for any device.

When we use the term embedded Linux, we mean that we use the Linux operating system on embedded systems, but embedded has different characteristics for the general purpose computing devices such as the following:

- Embedded systems have specific and dedicated applications

- Have limited memory, power, and storage capability

- They are almost always part of a larger system that may be linked to sensors or actuators

- They are embedded in automobiles, airplanes, and medical devices

- Works in real time (the outputs are directly related to its present inputs)

You can see embedded systems everywhere in everyday life. They can be found in vending machines, household appliances, smartphones, TVs, cars, parking systems, advanced driving assistance systems, and much more).

**Advantages and disadvantages of Embedded Linux**

• The Linux operating system is an efficient and scalable OS that can run on everything from low–cost devices to expensive large servers.

• Linux has a huge number of open source applications and tools.

• Open source = free.

•**Its only disadvantage** is that it cannot deal with real time applications due to the operating system overhead. So if you develop fast- response applications , like analog signal processing , embedded Linux will not be the best choice , but in special cases it can handle the real time systems using embedded Linux.

## Booting the Raspberry Pi

If you boot your desktop computer, you will see the Unified Extensible Firmware Interface (UEFI), which provides legacy support for BIOS (Basic Input/Output System) services. The Boot menu displays the system information and you can change the setting by pressing any key. UEFI tests the hardware of your computers like the memory, the hard disk, and then loads the operating system from the solid state drive (SSD). When a desktop computer is powered on , the UEFI/BIOS performs these steps:

1. Takes control of the processor of your computer

2. Tests the hardware components

3. Loads the operating system from your hard drive

## Raspberry Pi Bootloaders

Like any embedded Linux device, the Raspberry PI does not have a
BIOS by default. Indeed, it uses a combination of Bootloaders.
Bootloaders are programs used to link your hardware to your operating
system.

• Check the controllers such as the memory, I/O

• Prepare the memory for the operating system

• Load the operating system passing the control to it


In the following illustration you can find the sequence of the booting
process on the Raspberry Pi.

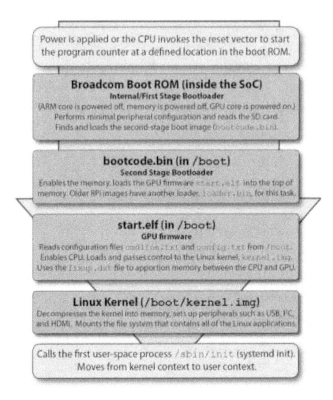

Power is applied or the CPU invokes the reset vector to start the program counter at a defined location in the boot ROM.

**Broadcom Boot ROM (inside the SoC)**
Internal/First Stage Bootloader
(ARM core is powered off, memory is powered off, GPU core is powered on.)
Performs minimal peripheral configuration and reads the SD card.
Finds and loads the second-stage boot image (bootcode.bin).

**bootcode.bin (in /boot)**
Second Stage Bootloader
Enables the memory, loads the GPU firmware start.elf into the top of memory. Older RPi images have another loader, loader.bin, for this task.

**start.elf (in /boot)**
GPU firmware
Reads configuration files cmdline.txt and config.txt from /boot.
Enables CPU. Loads and passes control to the Linux kernel, kernel.img.
Uses the fixup.dat file to apportion memory between the CPU and GPU.

**Linux Kernel (/boot/kernel.img)**
Decompresses the kernel into memory, sets up peripherals such as USB, I²C, and HDMI. Mounts the file system that contains all of the Linux applications.

Calls the first user-space process /sbin/init (systemd init).
Moves from kernel context to user context.

- Also, you can find the same information using the command dmesg | more in the terminal.

## Kernel and User Space

- The kernel space is the area that the Linux kernel runs in. It's an area of the system memory, but the area that regular applications run in is called user space, and there is a hard boundary between the kernel and the user space; this is to prevent the kernel from crashing, in case the user wrote bad code.

- The Linux kernel has the full access of the physical recourse, including memory on the Raspberry PI board.

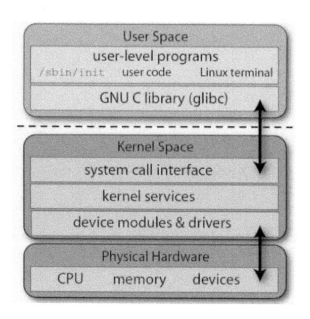

**More commands on Linux (some system commands)**

**systemct1 :** Lists all running services.

**systemect1 start ntp:** Starts a service. Does not persist after reboot.

**systemct1 stop ntp:** Stops a service. Does not persist after reboot.

**systemct1 enable ntp:** Enables a service to start on boot.

**systemct1 disable ntp:** Disables a service from starting on boot.

**systemct1 reload ntp:** Reloads configuration files for a service starting on boot.

● **The Super User** on Linux = the system administrator who has the highest level of security access to all commands. You can use the terminal as a super user by typing the **sudo passwd root** command.

**Let's create a new user on the Raspberry Pi**

**Called USER**

**Open the terminal window and write the following commands**:

pi@erpi- $ sudo adduser USER

Adding the user 'USER' . . .

Adding new group 'USER' (1002) . . .

 Adding new user 'USER' (1001) with group 'USER' . . .

Creating home directory '/home/USER' . . .

Copying files from 'etc/skel' . . .

Enter new UNIX password: enter your password

Retype new UNIX password: enter your password

Passwd: password updated successfully

**Git version control**

Git is a system that allows you to track your changes of the software you are developing.

There are two types of version control systems:

- Distributed: Like Git. Using such systems, you cannot pull down changes but you can clone the entire repository. "Clone" means copy, and it can become the master copy if required.

- Centralized: Like Apache (SVN), works on systems like that where you will find a master copy of your project, and then you can pull down changes.

For more details you can check out git.kernel.org

## Questions for Chapter 3

1.  What is embedded Linux?

2.  Create a user called "your name" on the Raspberry Pi.

3.  Describe the concept of version controls and its types.

4.  List the sequence of the booting process on the Raspberry Pi.

# Chapter 4

# Working with Electronics

**What you will learn in this chapter:**

Raspberry Pi boards

**What you will need for this chapter:**

Understanding the basics of electronics components

Interfacing electronics with the Raspberry Pi

## Electronics components

### Digital Multimeter

DMM is an electrical device used to measure the voltage, current, and resistance of a circuit.

If you don't have one, buy one that has the following features:

● **Auto range:** To automatically detect the range of the measurements.

● **Auto power off:** To save power and not waste your battery.

● **True RMS:** A multimeter with this feature uses real calculations to analyze phase-controlled devices like solid state drives.

## Introduction to electric circuits

● **Ohm's Law→ V = I X R**

This is the most important equation you will need.

● **V** for **Voltage**. Voltage is the potential difference between two points on a circuit. For example, if you have a buffer tank of water which is connected to the tap, water will flow if you turn on the tap because the height of the tank and the gravity, but if the tap was at the same height as the top of the water tank, water wouldn't flow because in this case there is no potential energy. Voltage also exhibits the same behavior; if the one side has a higher voltage than the other side , the current will flow across the component.

● **I for Current.** Measured in amperes (A), current is the flow of the electrical charge. Like in the water tank example, the current will be the flow of the water from the tank to the tap.

● **R for Resistance** (R). Resistance is measured in ohms ($\Omega$), and is something that reduces the flow of current through the dissipation of the power; power(P) in watts(W), P = V X I.

For example if you want to buy a resistor that limits the current to 100mA using a 5v supply, you can calculate it as the following $R = V$ $R/(IR = 5 \text{ V})/(100 \text{ mA}) = \textbf{50 } \boldsymbol{\Omega},$ and the power will be $P = VI = 0.5W.$

● *The total resistance of the series resistors = R1 + R2 + ... + Rn*

● *The voltage across the same resistor V supply= Vr1 + Vr2 + .... + Vr3*

Let's implement Raspberry Pi circuits on a breadboard.

We will use a breadboard for prototyping circuits, and in the next circuit we will use two horizontal power rails for 3.3V and 5V power. The Raspberry Pi GPIO headers consist of male pins, so you will need to use female jumper connectors for wiring the circuit.

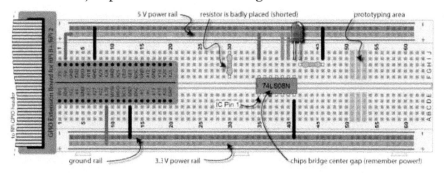

● Connect the circuit as shown in the above figure.

**Digital multimeters and the breadboard**

● We can measure the voltage on the circuit by connecting the multimeter in parallel (black probe in the COM).

● If you want to measure the current on the circuit you should insert the multi-meter between the components

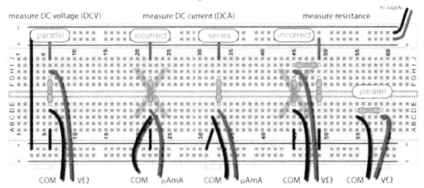

● A voltage regulator is a device that takes the varying input voltage and outputs a constant voltage, the Raspberry Pi B+ and Raspberry Pi 2/3 models have a dual efficiency PWM DC TO DC converter that can apply different fixed voltage levels on-board if there is a 5v, 3.3v and a 1.8v output. You can use the 5v and 3.3v on the Raspberry Pi GPIO headers, and the board can support up to 300mA on the 5v (pins 2 and 4).

And 50mA on the 3.3v pins (pins 1 and 17).

● If you want a larger current, you can use an external regulator which is used for components like motors.

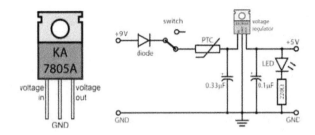

A diode is a semiconductor that allows the current to pass in one direction.

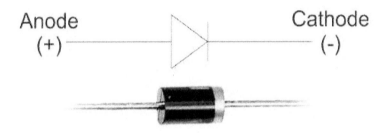

Light Emitting Diode (LED)

A light emitting diode is a semiconductor-based light source used mainly for debugging purposes.

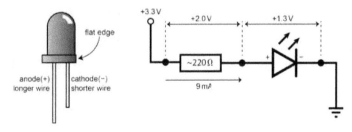

## Capacitor

A capacitor is an electrical component used to store electrical energy.

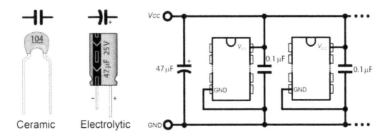

Ceramic     Electrolytic

- The first number is the first digit for the value.

- The second number is the second digit for the value.

- The third number is the number of zeros.

**For example:**

$104 = 100000pF = 100nF = 0.1\mu F$

## Transistors

Transistors are one of the core components of any microprocessor or any electronic system. We use transistors to amplify a signal on or off. You can also use it as a switch.

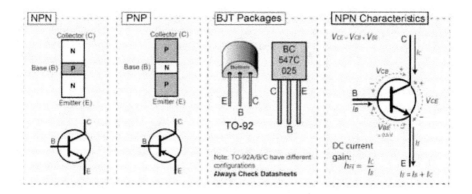

# Questions for Chapter 4

1. Explain Ohm's Law.

2. What is resistance?

3. What are the benefits of using regulators?

4. Describe how a diode works.

# Chapter 5

# Programming a  Raspberry Pi

**What you will learn in this chapter:**

Programming the Raspberry Pi using different languages

The difference between the compiler and interpreter

An intro to Python programming

 **What you will need for this chapter:**

Raspberry Pi board

Resistors, a breadboard, LEDs, transistors

## Introduction

In this chapter we will use many programming languages for the Raspberry Pi, including scripting and compiling languages. Take a look at the structure and syntax of each language and the advantages and disadvantages of each language (with examples), but we will mainly focus on the Python programming language.

Any programming language available on Linux will be also available on the Raspberry Pi , then you can choose the suitable language depending on the kind of application you are developing.

If you would like to do any of the following:

• Write device drivers for Linux

• Develop graphical user interfaces

• Design web applications

• Design a mobile application

Each choice will impact the option of the suitable language needed for that particular task, but there is a difference between the development for embedded systems and the development for other platforms like desktop, web, or mobile applications when you are developing for the embedded system. You should keep the following in mind:

- You should write clean code.

- You should optimize the code only if you complete it.

- You should have a good understanding of the hardware you are developing on.

**Languages on the Raspberry Pi**

By now you must be thinking, "What programming language should I use on the Raspberry Pi to guarantee the best performance?" Actually, this is a fairly difficult question to answer because, as we said before, it depends on what type of the application you are developing.

- Interpreted: The source code won't be translated directly to machine code, but the interpreter will read your code and then execute it line by line.

- Compiled: The compiler will translate the language directly to the machine code (0s and 1s).

- JIT: Just in time compiled means it has the feature of the compiled language, which is translating the source code directly into machine code. It also has the interpreter language, which is translated into the code line by line.

Also you may use Cython, this allow you to generate C code from your Python code. We will show some examples using Cython and the extended version of Python.

**Write the following commands on the terminal if you want to set the CPU frequency.**

$sudo apt install cpufrequtils

$cpufreq-info

**Set clock freq write the following commands.**

$sudo cpufreq-set -g performance

$cpufreq-info

$sudo cpufreq-set –f 700MHz

$cpufreq-info

**Example: Driving an LED with Raspberry Pi pins using transistors (wiring).**

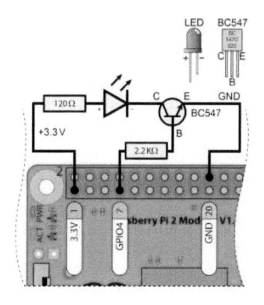

**Example: Driving an LED with Raspberry Pi pins using transistors.**

After wiring the circuit as shown, you can use Linux to control the Raspberry Pi pins with the following code:

```
$ cd /system/class/gpio

/system/class/gpio $ ls

/system/class/gpio $ echo 4 > export

/system/class/gpio $ ls

/system/class/gpio $ cd gpio4

/system/class/gpio/gpio4 $ ls
```

**Now it's time to control GPIO4:**

/system/class/gpio/gpio4 $ echo out > direction

/system/class/gpio/gpio4 $ echo 1 > value

/system/class/gpio/gpio4 $ echo 0 > value

A scripting language is a type of computer programming that is used to write scripts that are interpreted directly with no compiler.

**There are many types like:**

● **Python**: It's a great and very easy language to learn and use for scripting and object-oriented support features.

● **Bash**: A good choice for short tasks and you don't need advanced programming structures.

● **Perl**: You can use this language for text or process data. It allows you to write code in object-oriented paradigms.

● **Lua**: This scripting language is used a lot with embedded applications. It is a lightweight language and supports object-oriented programming styles.

**Example: Drive the LED using Bash.**

LED-IO = 5 # use a variable called LED with value 5

Function blinkLED

{

  Echo $1 >> "/sys/class/gpio/gpio$LED_IO/value"

}

If [$# -ne 1]; then

echo "No command has been entered".

echo " on or off "

echo –e " setup the LED "

exit 2

if

echo"The command has been entered is $1"

```
if ["$1" == "setup"]; then

echo "IO $1"

echo "the LED is on"

echo $LED_IO >> "sys/class/IO/export"

sleep 1

echo "away" >> "sys/class/IO$LED_IO/direction"

elif ["$1" == "on"]; then

echo "LED is on"

blinkLED 1

elif ["$1" == "off"]; then

echo "LED is off"

blinkLED 0

elif [$1 == "status"]; then

state=$(cat "/sys/class/IO/IO$LED/value")

echo "LED State is: $state"

elif ["$1" == "end"]; then

echo"Io num $LED_IO"

echo $LED_IO >> "/sys/class/IO/unexport"

fi
```

**Example: Drive the LED using Lua.**

```lua
local LED4_PIN = "sys/class/IO/IO4"

local SYSFS_DIR = "sys/class/IO/"

local LED_Num = "4"

function writeIO(dir, filen, val)

file = IO.open(dir..filen,"w")

file:write(val)

file:close()

end

print("Driving the LED")

ifarg[1] == nil then

print("you should enter a command")

print(" usage is: command")

print("1 -> on or 0-> off")

do return en

end

if arg[1] == "off" then

print("The LED is on")
```

```
wirteIO("LED4_PIN", "val", "1")

elseif arg[1] == "configure "then

print("the LED is off")

WirteIO(LED4_PIN, "val", "0")

Elesif arg[1] == "configure"

Print("configure the IO")

WriteIO(SYSFS_DIR, "xport", LED_NUM)

Os.execute()

WriteIO(LED4_PIN,"DIR","out")

Elseif arg[1]=="sta"then

Print("turn IO off"

Print("find the LED sta")

File=io.open(LED4_PIN.."val","r")

File:close()

Else

Print("please insert a valid command")

End

Print("the end")
```

**Example: Drive the LED using Python.**

```
Import sys

From time import sleep

LED4_PIN = "/sys/class/IO/IO4"

SYS_DIR = "/sys/class/IO"

LED_NUM = "4"


def wLED(fname, val, PIN = LED4_PIN)

"This function to set the value on the file"

Fileo = open(PIN + fname,"w")

Fileo.write(val)

Fileo.close()

Return


Print("start the script")

If len(sys.argv) !=4

Print("incorrect argument")

Sys.exit(4)

If.argv[1]=="on"
```

```
Print("the LED is on")

wLED(fname="val", val="1")

elif sys.argv[1] =="turn off"

 print("The LED is off")

wLED(fname="val", val="0")

elif sys.argv[1]=="configure":

print("configure the IO")

wLED(fname="xport", val="LED_NUM", PIN=SYS_DIR)

sleep(0.1)

wLED(fname="DIR", val="out")

eleif sys.argv[1] == "close"

print("The IO I off")

wLED(fname="unexport", val=LED_NUM, PIN=SYS_DIR)

eleif sys.argv[1]=="state"

print("the LED state")

fileo = open(LED4_PIN + "val", "r")

print(fileo.read())

fileo.close()

else

print("please enter a valid command")
```

```
print("end of the script")
```

## Questions of Chapter 5

1. What is the object-oriented paradigm?

2. Define the difference between compiled and interpreted languages.

3. Write python code to turn on an LED on GPIO 4 60 times in one minute.

# Chapter 6

# Input and output on a Raspberry pi

**What you will learn in this chapter:**

Interfacing on a Raspberry Pi

PWM concepts

The importance of pull up and pull down resistors

**What you will need for this chapter:**

Raspberry Pi board

Buttons, transistors

LEDs

## Introduction

In this chapter you will use what you have learned in the five previous chapters about Linux, programming, and electronics basics, so you will start working with the general purpose inputs/outputs on the Raspberry Pi, as well as work with Pulse Width Modulation (PWM). At the end, you will work with the Wiring Pi Library, so let's get started...

After showing you how to administrate Linux and practice different commands on the command line, building electronic circuits, and programming using different languages it's now time to integrate all of these things to control the Raspberry Pi in different ways like:

- Using the buses, for example SPI and I2C.

- Using UART on the GPIO.

- Communicating through Wi-Fi or Bluetooth with electronic components.

- Connecting your USB devices like keyboards, Wi-Fi modules, etc.

Now we will use the GPIO header to connect the Raspberry Pi to circuits. The next example will provide you a view of the functions of the GPIO header, you will find that many of the pins are multiplexed, which means that the same pin can do more than one.

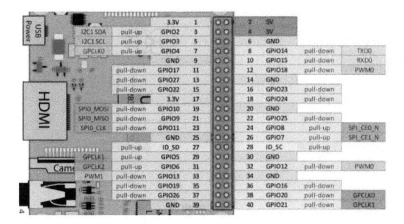

## General Purpose Inputs/ Outputs

## You can use them for the following purpose:

● **Digital input:** In this case, you can read a digital output from an electronic device/circuit.

● **Analog output:** You can use Pulse width modulation to output a signal that can be used as a voltage level to control devices like servo motors.

● **Digital output:** You can use a GPIO to turn the circuit on or to turn it off, for example when you use an LED or a relay (switch) to turn on/off high voltage devices.

● **Analog input:** You cannot use this feature (ADC) directly on the Raspberry Pi, but you can add it using bus devices.

### General purpose input/output digital output

In this example we used a GPIO to connect a FET to the switch circuit.

When the voltage is applied to the gate, it will close the switch to enable the current to flow from 5 volts using the 220 ohm resistor. This is applied on the right-hand side picture, and you can use this circuit for many on/off output and input applications because the BS270FET can drive a constant current up to 400mA.

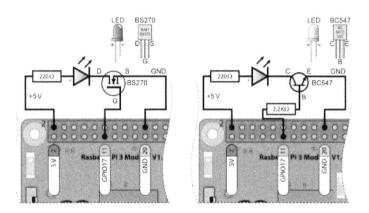

**Now let's test the performance of this circuit using a short bash shell script to control the LED.**

**Write the following:**

echo  17 > /sys/class/gpio/export

sleep 0.7

echo "" > /sys/class/gpio/gpio7/direction

count = 0

while [ $count –lt 100000]; do

echo 1 > /sys/class/gpio/gpio17/val

let count = count +1

echo 0 > /sys/class/gpio/gpio17/value

58

done

echo 17 > /sys/class/gpio/unexport

This is the reading of output signal on an oscilloscope:

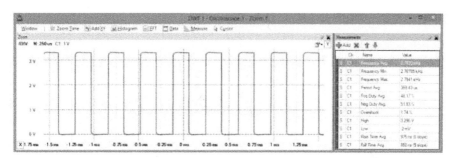

## General purpose input/output digital input

In this example we will apply the concept of GPIO digital input.

The GPIO digital input will allow us to read the state of a pushbutton or any on/off input (0 or 1) we will use both the Linux terminal and C++ to perform this task. The circuit in the following figures use normal pushbuttons (SPST) that are connected to the Raspberry Pi pin 13/GPIO27. You will not need pull-up or pull-down resistors on pushbutton switches because pin 13 on the GPIO header is directly consented to ground using an internal resistor (pull down resistor).

Open the Linux terminal and write the following:

/sys/class/gpio/$ echo 27 >export

/sys/class/gpio/$ c gpio twenty seven

/sys/class/gpio/gpiotwentyseven $ ls

/sys/class/gpio/gpiotwentyseven $echo in > direction

/sys/class/gpio/gpiotwentyseven $ cat direction in

/sys/class/gpio/gpiotwentyseven $ cat value 0

/sys/class/gpio/gpiotwentyseven $ cat value 1

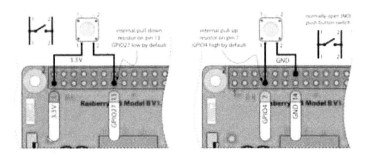

## The pull down and pull up resistors

● **Pull up resistor**: From its name, it pulls the voltage of the wire that connected to its source when the other components on the line are inactive, and they are disconnected.

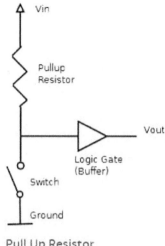

Vin

Pullup
Resistor

Vout

Logic Gate
(Buffer)

Switch

Ground

Pull Up Resistor

- **Pull down resistor:** It works like the pull up resistor, but it's connected to the ground and holds the signal when the other devices are disconnected.

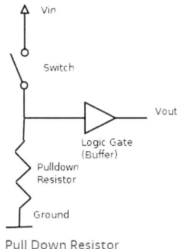

Pull Down Resistor

## Control the GPIOs using C++

There is a C++ class with the sysfs GPIO functions on the Raspberry Pi to make it much easier to use. You transfer it to any embedded Linux device. There is another approach called memory-mapped that you will see at the end of the chapter, but keep in mind that all of these approaches are specific to the Raspberry Pi board.

#define GPIO_Address "/sys/class/gpio"

Namespace Raspberry {

enum GPIO_DIR{IN, OUT};

enum GPIO_VAL {low=0, HIGH=1};

enum GPIO_EDGE {none, rise, fall, both}

```
};


Class GPIO {

private:

int number, debounceTime;

string name, address;

public:

GPIO(int number);

Virtual int getNumber() {return number;}


// input and output configurations

Virtual int setDir(GPIO_DIR);

Virtual GPIO_DIR getDIR();

Virtual int setVal(GPIO_VAL);

Virtual int toggleOut();

Virtual GPIO_VAL getVal ();

Virtual int setActivelow(bool is low=true);

Virtual int setAciveHigh();

Virtual void setDebounceTime(int time)

{this-> debounceTime = time;
```

```
}
};
// Advanced, faster by open the stream
Virtual int streamopen();

Virtual int streamWrite(GPIO_VAL);

Virtual int streamClose();

Virtual int toggleOut(int time);

Virtual int toggleOut(int numOfTime, int time);

Virtual void changeToggTime(int time)


{
  This->threadRunning =false;
}
// input
Virtual int setEdgeType(IO_EDGE);

Virtual IO_EDGE getEdge();

Virtual int waitEdge();

Virtual int waitEdge(callbackType callback);

Virtual void waitEdgeClose(){this->threadRunning = false;}

Virtual ~IO(); // destructor
```

Private:

Int write(string address, string fname, string val);

Int write (string address, string fname, int val);

string read(string address, string fname);

int exportIO();

int unexportIO();

of stream;

thr_t thread;

callbackType callbackfunc;

bool thrRunning;

int togglePer;

int toggleNum;

friend void* thrpoll(void *val);

};


Void* thrpoll(void *val);

Void* thrtogg(void *val);

}/* namespace Raspberry*/


File c++control.cpp

```cpp
#include<iostream>

#include<unistd.h> //for usleep function

#include"GPIO.h"

Using namespce Raspberry

Using namespace std;

Int main()

{

GPIO outIO(17);

outIO.setDIR(OUT);


for(int I =0; I <10; i++)

{

  outIO.setVal(HIGH);

usleep(400000);

outIO.setVal(LOW);

usleep(400000);

}

inIO.setDIR(INPUT);

cout << "input state is"<<inIO.getVal() <<endl;

outIOlstreamOpen()
```

```
for(int i =0; I < 100000000; i++)

{

  outIO.streamWrite(HIGH);

outIO.streamWrite(LOW);

}

outIO.close();

return 0;
```

In the following figure you will see the performance of the code when the write() method is used; it is flashing at 129 kHz.

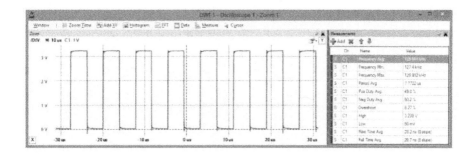

**POSIX**

Ptherads is a set of functions written in the C language to allow you to implement threads with C/C++ programs. You will need threads when you want to run some parts of your code at the same time.

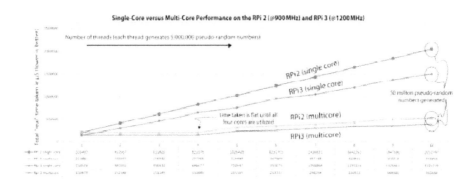

## Pulse Width Modulation - LED Fading

The Raspberry Pi has the capability (PWM) to provide analog to digital conversion (DAC), which is usually used for motor devices.

All Raspberry Pi boards have Pulse Width Modulation pins.

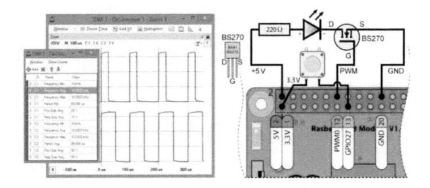

We will use the PWM feature to fade an LED by changing the duty cycle value.

Create file call LEDFading.cpp.

Then write the following code:

```cpp
#include <iostream>

#include <wiringPi.h>

#include <unistd.h>

Using namespace std;

#define LED_PIN 18

#define Button_PIN 27

Bool run  = true;

Void buttPress(void)
```

```
{
  Cout<< "you pressed the Button";

Run = false

}

Int main ()

{
  wiringPiSetupIO();

pinMode(LED_PIN, OUTPUT);

pinMode(Button_PIN, INPUT);

wirinPisr(Button_PIN, INT_EDGE_Rise, &buttPress);

cout << "LED fading until the button is pressed";

while(run)

{
  For (int I =1; I <=1023; i++)

{
  pmWrite(LED_PIN, i);

usleep(1000);

}
  for(int i=1022; i>=0; i--)

{
```

```
   pmWrite(LED_PIN, i);

usleep(1000);      //delay

}

}

return 0;

}


}
```

## Questions for Chapter 6

1. Describe the difference between pull-up and pull-down resistors.

2. What is Pulse Width Modulation? How many pins are on the Raspberry Pi?

3. List the purposes of using the general input output pin on the Raspberry Pi.

4. Using C++, write a program to control servo motors using the PWM pin on the Raspberry Pi.

5. What is the benefit of using POSIX?

# Chapter 7

# Introduction to Communication Protocols

**What you will learn in this chapter:**

Understand bus communication

More code with C/C++

**What you will need for this chapter:**

Raspberry Pi board

Seven segment display

Shift register

**Introduction**

In this chapter you will work with the following communication protocols:

- SPI: serial peripheral interface

- I2C: inter integrated circuit

- UART: Universal Asynchronous Receiver/Transmitter

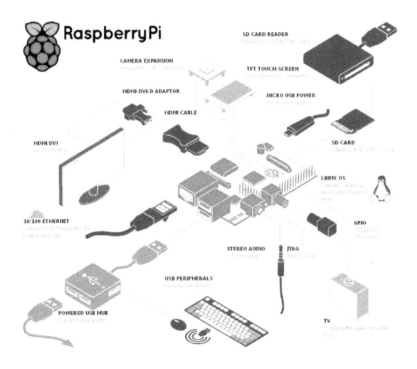

## I2C

The I2C protocol or IIC is a protocol with two wires that were invented by the Philips company. The benefit of this protocol is to connect microcontrollers with other peripheral devices. You can use it with the Raspberry Pi for the following reasons::

● The Raspberry Pi will act as the master device.

● The other devices will connect to the Raspberry Pi and will act as slaves on the same wire.

### The Advantages of using I2C

● You can implement the I2C using just two signal lines for communication, which is the serial data and the serial clock.

- **Serial data:** to transfer the data

- **Serial clock:** to synchronize the data transfer

● Any device on the bus can be a master or a slave.

  - Master device: the device that can initiate communication

  - Slave device: the device that can respond

● There is a built-in chip for noise filtering.

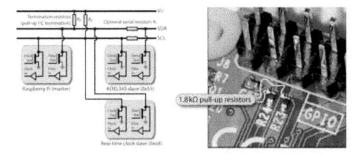

●On the Raspberry Pi, the IIC was implemented using the Broadcom controller, which supports up to 400,000 Hz. NXP has a new one which supports up to 1,000,000 Hz.

● You can see the pull up resistors on the serial data and the serial clock. They are used as termination resistors; they enable the master device to take control of the bus with the slaves.

To configure the I2C on the Raspberry Pi, open the terminal and write the following:

Config.txt | grep i2c_arm

Then save and restart; let's make it available.

After the restart, open the terminal and write the following:

Sudo modprobe i2c-bcm2708

Sudo modprobe i2c-dev

Lsmod | grep i2c

## On the Raspberry Pi you will find the following I2C buses:

I2C1: Serial data on PIN3, Serial clock on PIN5, not enabled by default.

I2C0: Serial data on PIN27, Serial clock on PIN28, this is used for HAT management.

To change the baud rate, open the terminal and then write the following:

Sudo cat /sys/module/i2c_bcm2708/parameter/baudrate

**Reboot and then write the following**

Sudo cat /sys/module/i2c_bcm2708/parameter/baudrate 4000

## I2C in C programming

This program can be run on any i2c device.

```c
#include<stdio.h>

#include<fcnt1.h>

#include<sys/ioct1.h>

#include<Linux/i2c.h>

#include<Linux/i2c-dev.h>

#define size 19

Int bTOD (char b)

{

return (b/16)*10 + (b%16);

}
```

```
Int main()

{

  Int file;

 Printf("test is starting \n");

If(file=open("/dev/i2c-1", o_RDWR < 0)

{

  perror(" cannot open your bus\n ");

 return 1;

}

 If(ioct1(file, I2C_SLAVE, 0x68) < 0)

{

Perror ("cannot connect the sensor");

Return 1;

}

Char writeBuff[1] = {0x00};

If (write(file, writeBuff, 1)!=1

{

Perror("Failed to set your entered address\n");

Return 1;

}
```

```
Char buff(Size);

If(read(file, buff, Size)!=Size)

{

  Perror("Failed to your data in the buffer\n");

}

Printf("Time is %02d:%02d:%02d\n", bTOD(buff[0]));

Float temp = buff[0x11] + ((buff [0x12] >>6)*0.25);

Printf("the temp : %f\n", temp);

Close(file);

Return 1;

}
```

## SPI BUS

SPI stands for Serial Peripheral Interface. It's a fast, full duplex serial data link that allows devices like the Raspberry Pi to communicate with other devices, but in short distances, so such as I2C the SPI Protocol is also synchronous. But I2c is not a full duplex bus unlike the SPI, so if you use SPI you can send and receive the data at the same time. We will use the SPI bus to drive a seven segment LED Display using an 8-bit shift register.

Now let's take a look at the differences between IIC and SPI.

**IIC**: Two wires, 128 devices can be attached. **SPI**: Four wires, and also needs to connect it with logic if you want to attach more than one slave device.

**IIC**: It uses half duplex with 400000Hz. **SPI**: It uses full duplex with 32MHz.

**IIC**: You will need to connect pull-up resistors. **SPI**: There is no need for pull-up resistors.

**IIC**: The most important feature is that you can have multiple masters. **SPI:** Very simple but no more than one master device.

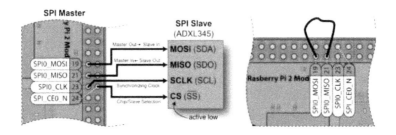

SPI bus works using one of the four modes that are chosen based on the specification defined in the data sheet of the SPI device. The data can be synchronized by the clock signal and any of the communication modes. The polarity can be defined if the clock is low or high.

**SPI Modes**

**Mode**: 0, **polarity**: 0 (low), **clock Phase**: 0

**Mode**: 1, **polarity**: 0 (low), **clock Phase**: 1

**Mode**: 2, **polarity**: 1 (high), **clock Phase**: 0

**Mode**: 3, **polarity**: 1 (high), **clock Phase**: 1

• There is no defined maximum data rate with the SPI protocol, also no flow control, and no communication acknowledgement.

**Raspberry Pi and SPI Protocol**

The GPIO header on the Raspberry Pi that has the SPI bus is disabled by default, but you can enable the bus by the following steps:

• Add an entry to the file /boot/config.txt/etc/modules

Cat config.txt | grep spi

Cat modules | grep spi

Sudo reboot

Ls spi*

**SPI application (seven segment display)**

The seven segment display consists of eight LEDs that can be used to display decimal or hexadecimal numbers. There are many types with different colors and sizes.

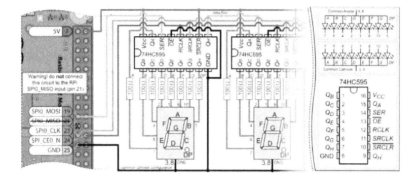

The 74HC595 can be connected to the Raspberry Pi board using three of the four SPI lines.

● Connect the SPI0_CLK to the Serial clock input (pin 11) of the 74HC595.

● The benefit of SPI0_MOSI is to transfer the data from the Raspberry Pi to the 74HC595 Serial input (pin 14). You can send 8 bits at a time.

● SPI_CE0_N is connected to the Register Clock input to latch the 74HC595 to the output pins to light the LEDs.

## The SPI Communication in C programming

#include <stdio.h>

#include<cnt1.h>

#include<unistd.h>

#include<stdint.h>

```c
#include<linuxspi/spidev.h>

#define SPI_ADDRESS "/dev/spidev0 .0"

Const unsigned char symb[16]=

{

 0b0011111, 0b00000110, 0b01011011, ob1001111,

 0b01100110, 0b01101101, 0b01111101, 0b00000111,

0b01111111, 0b01100111, 0b01110111, 0b01111100,

0b00111001, 0b01011110, 0b01111001, 0b01110001

};

Int transferData(int lg, unsigned char se, unsigned char rc[], int le)

Struct spi_ioc transfer trans;

Transfer.txx_buff = (unsigned long) se;

Transfer.rx_buff = (unsigned long) rc;

Transfer.le = le;

Transfer.speed_hez = 1000000; // speed in herz

Transfer.b_per_w = 8; // bits per word

Transfer.del_us = 0; // delay in micro second

Transfer.cx_change = 0; //chip affect transfer

Transfer.tx_nbits=0; //no bits for writing

Transfer.rx_nbits=0; //no bits for reading
```

```
Transfer.pd = 0; //interbyte delay

Int status = ioct1 (lg, SPI_IOC_MESSAGE(1), &transfer);

If(status < 0)

{

  Perror ("*SPI: SPI_IOC_MESSAG Failed ");

Return -1;

}

  Return status;

}

Int main () {

  Unsigned int lg, I; //file to handle and loop counter

  Unsigned char null=0x00; // only sending one char

  Unit8_t mode = 3;    //SPI mode


If (lg = open(SPI_ADDRESS, o_RDWR) <0 )

{

  Perror ("SPI Error: cannot open the device");

Return -1;

}

If (ioct1 (lg, SPI_IOC_RD_MODE, &MODE)==-1)
```

```
{

 Perror("SPI: Cannot set the mode of SPI");

 Return -1;

 }

If(ioctl(lg, SPI_TOC_WR_MODE, &mode)==-1))

 {

  Perror("SPI: Cannot get the mode of SPI");

 Return -1;

 }

Printf("SPI Mode: %d\n", mode);

Printf("count in hexa from 0 to F");




For(i=0; i<=15; i++)

 {

  // this code to receive and send the data

 If(transfer(lg, (unsigned char*), &symb[i], &null, 1)==-1)

 Perror ("cannot update the display");

 Return -1;
```

}

Printf("%5d\r", i); //print the nun in the terminal window

fflush(stout); // flus the output

usleep(60000) // delay for 600ms  in each loop

}

Close(lg);

Return 0;

}

You can use the ioct1() function to override the current settings of the device, but if you add xx you can read and write.

●SPI_IOC_XX_MOE: The transfer mode of SPI (0-3)

● SPI_IOC_XX_BITS_PER_WORD: determine the number of bits in each word

● SPI_IOC_XX_LSB_FIRST: 0 is MSB, 1 is LSB

● SPI_TOC_XX_MAX_SPEED_HZ: to set the max transfer rate in Hz

**UART**

UART stands for Universal Asynchronous Receiver/Transmitter. It's a microprocessor peripheral device that is used for serial data transfer, one bit at a time, between any two devices. UART was once a standalone IC, but it is now integrated with the host microcontroller. A UART is described as asynchronous because the sender can't send a clock signal to the recipient to synchronize the transmission. Usually the data is sent by only two lines such as your telephone line that uses the transmit data connection (TXD) and the receive data connection (RXD). It's very common to use the logic level for the UART outputs and inputs to enable two UARTs to connect with each other.

The number of symbols per second is called the baud rate, or modulation rate; the symbol could be two bits, so the byte rate will be $1/8^{th}$ of the bit rate.

This figure represents UART transmission format for one byte.

On the Raspberry Pi you will find the following:

A full UART that you can access via the GPIO header.

- TXD0 (pin8): to transmit data to a receiver

- RXD0 (pin 10): to receive data from a transmitter

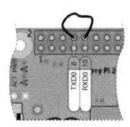

The /dev directory has an entry for ttAMA0. This is the terminal device, which is a software interface that enables you to send and receive data.

## Advantages and disadvantage of UART communication

● Very simple wire transmissions with error checking, **but** the max data rate is very low compared to others like SPI.

● Easy to implement for interconnecting embedded devices and PCs, **but** the clock on both devices must be accurate especially at high baud rate.

● Can be interfaced to RS physical interfaces to enable long distance communication more than 15 meters, **but** you need to know the UART settings in advance like the baud rate, size, and checking type.

## UART in C Programming

```
#include <stdio.h>

#include<fcnt1.h>

#include<unistd.h>

#include<termios.h>

Include<string.h>


Int main(int argc, char *argv[])

{

  Int myFile, myCount;
```

```
If(argc!=2)

{

 Printf("please enter a string to your program\n");

Return -2;

}

If(myFile =open("/dev/ttAMA0", O_RDWR | O_noctty |
O_NDELAY) < 0  )

{

  Perror ("cannot open the device");

Return -1}

Struct termios options;

Tcgetarr(file, &options);

Options.c_cflag = b115200 | cs8 | CREAD | CLOAL;

Options.c_iflag = IGNPAR | ICRNL;

Tcflush(myFile, TCANOW, &options);

Tcflush(myFile, TCLFULUSH)

Tcsetattr(file, TCSANOW, &options);

If(count = write(myFile, argv[1], strlen(1)))<0)

{

 Perror("UART: cannot write to the output\n");

Return -1;
```

```
}
```

Write(myFile, "\n\r",2);

Close(myFile);

Return 0;

```
}
```

In the above code we have used the termios structure.

The termios structure has many members:

- tcflag_t c_iflag: to set the input modes

- tcflag_t c_oflag: to set the output modes

- tcflag_t c_cflag: to set the control modes

- tcflag_t c_1flag: to set the local modes

- cc_T c_cc [NCCS]: Used for special characters

## Questions for Chapter 7

1. Compare IIC and SPI.

2. Define UART.

3. Implement the UART in C.

4. List the advantages of SPI.

# Chapter 8

# Python Programming for the Raspberry Pi

**What you will learn in this chapter:**

Start programming with Python

 Use Python for automation

Drive the hardware with Python

**What you will need for this chapter:**

Raspberry Pi board

## Introduction to Python Programming

In this chapter you will learn how to use Python to develop basic encryption, user input, and graphical user interfaces.

Let's start with the "hello world" example as in any programming language.

Create a file named hello.py using the nano text editor.

Nano –c hello.py

Within the file write the following code:

```
#!/usr/bin/python3

#hello.py

Print ("Hello World")
```

After writing the code, save and exit. You can run the file using the following command:

Python3 hello.py

You should know more about strings if you want to start with Python.

A string is a sequence of characters stored together as a value. We will write code to get the user's input, using string manipulation to switch the letters and then print the encrypted message of the user input. You can use text editors that can be directly on your Raspberry Pi or via VNC or SSH. There are many text editors you can choose from:

• Nano: You can work with this editor from the terminal.

• IDLE3: This editor includes syntax highlighting and context help, but this program requires x-windows or x11 to run remotely. We will use Python 3, so make sure that you run IDL3 and not IDLE.

●Geany: This editor is an Integrated Development Environment (IDE) that supports many programming languages, syntax highlighting, auto completion, and very easy code navigation. This is a rich editor , but not for beginners and it will be slow on the Raspberry Pi. If you want to install Geany, write the following command:

 Sudo apt-get install Geany

To make sure that the Geany editor uses Python 3:

Click on the Execute button to run the code.  You will need to change the build commands. Load the file.

Click build and set build commands and then change Python to Python 3.

Let's create the program

```
#!/usr/bin/python3

#ecryptionprogram.py

#takes the input and encrypt it

def encrpytText(input_text,key);

output=""""

for letter in input_text:

#Ascii Uppercase 65-90 lowercase 97 -122

Ascii_val = ord(letter)
```

#now write the following code to exclude non characters from encryption

If(ord("A") > Ascii_val) or (Ascii_val > ord("Z")):

Output+=letter

Else:

#write this code to apply the encryption key

Key_val = Ascii_val + key

#make sure that we use A-Z regardless of key

If not((or("A")) < key_val < or("Z")):

 Key_val = ord("A") + (key_val-ord("A"))\

       %(ord("Z") –ord("A")+1)

#add the encrypted letter to the output

Output+=str(chr(key_val))

Return output

#Test

Def main()

Print ("please enter any text to encrypt")

#get user input

Try:

Us_input = input();

Sc_result = ecryptText(us_input, 10)

```
Print ("output: ", sc_result)

Print("to un-scramble , pls press enter")

Input()

Un_result = ecryptText(Sc_result, -10)

Print ("output: " + un_result)

Except UnicodeDecodeError:

Print ("this program supports ASCII characters only")

Main()

#end of the program
```

The preceding code implements a basic method to encode the text using a character substitution called the Caesar Cipher, named after Julius Caesar, who used this method to send his secret orders to the army.

We have defined two functions; encryptText() and main().

When the code is running, the main function contains the user's input using the input() command. The result is stored as a string in the us_ input variable.

```
Us_input = input()
```

● Keep in mind that the input() function can't handle non ASCII characters, so we will use try() function to solve this problem, which will cause UnicodeDecodeError.

We also call the encryptText() function with two parameters; the text to be encrypted, and the key. After that, the output will be printed.

Sc_result = ecryptText(us_input, 10)

Print("Output:" + Sc_result)

At the end, we will use input() to get the user input. The encryptText() will perform a simple form of encryption by shifting the position of the letters. That means substituting the letter with another letter based on the key; for example, if the letter is "A" and the key is 3 the output will be "D." This table shows you the idea of the Caesar Cipher.

In our example, "A" = 65, the key = 3, so the output = 65 +3 = 68 which is "D."

| A | B | C | D | E | F | G | H | I | J | K | L | M |
|----|----|----|----|----|----|----|----|----|----|----|----|----|
| 65 | 66 | 67 | 68 | 69 | 70 | 71 | 72 | 73 | 74 | 75 | 76 | 77 |
| N | O | P | Q | R | S | T | U | V | W | X | Y | Z |
| 78 | 79 | 80 | 81 | 82 | 83 | 84 | 85 | 86 | 87 | 88 | 89 | 90 |

After that, we will make sure that we have an empty string to build our result (output = ""), and then we will set our key to encrypt the text.

The input_text variable will contain strings that are stored as a list (a list is something like an array). You can access every item in the list using input_text[0] for the first item and so on. Python also allows you to loop through a list using the line of code for "item" in "items", to access each item.

The **letter in input_text**: This line allows you to break up the input by looping it through for each item inside and to set the letter equal to that, so if the input is equal to HELLO, it will run the code five times for H,E,L,L, and O. This allow you to read every letter separately, and then add the new encrypted letter to the output string.

The next line , if(ord("A) > Ascii_val) or (Ascii_val > ord("Z")):,

We write this line to check if the character we are looking at is not between A and Z, which means it is may be a number or a mark. In this case, the program will exclude the character from the encryption process (the output will not change).

If the letter is correct (between A and Z), you can add the value to our encryption key of 10 (Shifting 10 positions).

**Input**: A B C D E F G H I J K L M N O P Q R S T U V W X Y Z

**Output**: K L M N O P Q R S T U V W X Y Z A B C D E F G H I J

As you want the encrypted message to be much easier to write, you have a small output between A and Z, so if the letter starts with X, you want to wrap it and count from A. You can do this by writing the %(modulus) function, that gives you the remainder value of the input (if you divide a number by another number) if the number is 24, and if you add 10, you will get 34. The value of 34%26 (26 is the total number of the letters) is 8. Start from A until H.

In ASCII, the A is equal to the number 65, so you will remove the offset from the key_val and then add it once you have the modulus value. The next code makes sure that you limit the ASCII values to anything between A and Z:

#makes sure that you use A to Z regardless of key

If not((ord("A")) < key_val < ord("Z")):

Key_val = ord("A") + (key_val-or("A"))\

$$\%(ord("Z") -ord("A")+1)$$

If the entered value is not between the values for A or Z, then you will allow the value to wrap around (after calculating the modulus the total number of letters between A and Z, which is 26). This works if the key is larger than 26 and if you are counting in the opposite way, for example:

if the key was negative, the decryption key will be positive.

The following figure will show you the basic form of encryption, you will supply the method and the key to the one you want to read your message:

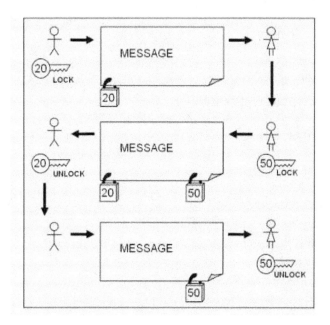

If you would like to send the message without the key and the method to the receiver, you will do the following as in the figure:

First, you will encrypt it and send the message over to the other one, and then they encrypt it again with their own encryption and send it back. The message at this point has two layers of the applied encryption. Now you can remove your encryption. At the end, the other side will receive the message with his/her encryption, which he/she can remove to read the message.

You should keep in mind that there are 25 encryption combinations.

You can run the file directly; Python will set _name_to the main global attribute with this code.

If __name__ ==”__main__”:

main()

Now let's create key.py and write the following code

#!/user/bin/python3

#key.py

Import encryptdecrypt as ENC

Key_1 = 20

Key_2 = 50

Print(“enter your text: ”)

#get user input

Us_input = input()

#send message

encodKey = ENC.encryptText(us_input, key_1)

print(us_1: send message encrypted with Key_1:” + encodKey)

encodKey2 = ENC.encryptText(encodKEY1KEY2, -KEY1)

print(“us_1: removes KEY1 & returns with KEY2(KEY2):” + encodKey2)

#Receiver will remove the encryption

Msg_res = ENC.encryptText(encodKEY2, -KEY2)

Print("us_2: will remove KEY2 & msg received :" + msg_res)

# End of the program

## Using files

In this part you will learn how to use and specify a file, via the command line, that will be read and encoded to produce the output file.

Now let's create a file named myFile.txt. Write the following code:

```
#!/user/bin/python3

#myfile.py

Import sys # to obtain command line parameters

Import encryptdecrypt as ENC

#define inputs

RG_IN = 1

RG_OUT = 2

RG_KEY = 3

RG_LEN = 4
```

```
def conv_File(in, out, key)

#convert the key to an integer

try:

encr_Key = int(key)

except ValueErr:

print("invalid: your key %s should be an integer" %(key))

#put it on to the lines

Else:

Try:

#open your files

With open(in) as f_in:

In_content = f_in.readlines()

Except IOError:

Print ("Unable to open %s" % (in))

try:

with open (out,'w') as f_out:

for line in in_content:

out_line = ENC.encryptText(line, enc_key)

f_out.writelines(out_line)
```

```python
except IOError:

print("cannot open %s %(in)")

try:

with open(out,'w') as f_out:

for line in in_content:

out_line = ENC.encryptText(line, en_key)

f_out.writelines(out_line)

except IOError:

print("cannot open %s" %(out))

print("the process is complete %s " %(out) )

finally:

print("complete")


#check the parameters

If len(sys.argv) == RG_LEN

Print("comm: %s" %(sys.argv))

convertFile(sys.argv[RG_IN], sys.argv[RG_OUT], sys.argv[RG_KEY])

else:

print("myFile.py in out key")

#End of the program
```

• To run the programs, write the following Python 3 myfile.py in the out key.

For instance, to encrypt myFile.txt and output it as encrypted.txt, use 20 as the key by writing the following command:

Python3 myfile.py in.txt encrypted.txt 20

If you want to show the result, use less encrypted.txt and enter Q to exit.

If you want to decrypt encrypted.txt and output it as decrypted.txt, use -20.

• Python myFile.py encrypted.txt decrypted.txt -20

This code requires us to use parameters that are provided in the terminal window. You will access them by importing the Python module called sys. Like you did before, you will also import your encrypt/decrypt module by the import command. You will use the part to allow you to refer to it using ENC.

Next, you will set the values to define what each command-line parameter will represent. If you run it , you will see that sys.argv[] is an array of values like in the following array:

['myfile.py', 'in.txt', 'encrypted.txt', '20']

So the input file will be at index 1 in the list, then the output file, and finally, the key with the total number of parameters RG_LEN = 4.

• Next, you will define the convertFile() function that you will call upon later from the next block of code.

• If you want to step away from errors, you will check if the length of the sys.argv value matches the number of parameters from the terminal window. This will make sure that the user has supplied you with enough, and you shouldn't try to reference items in the sys.argv[] list that don't exist. You will return a short message to explain what you are expecting.

• You will now call the convertFile() function via the terminal window values and making use of Python's built in exception handling features to ensure that errors are responded to accordingly.

• The line try/except code allow us to try to run some code and handle any exceptions (errors) in the program itself, and to halt any sudden stop.

The try code is accompanied by the following options:

• except valError: If an error occurs, a specific type of exception can be specified and handled with the action, depending on the error you wish to handle. For valError, you could check if the value is a float value and convert it to an integer or prompt for a new one. Multiple exceptions can be caught using except (valError, IOError) as required.

• except: This is to catch all cases of any possible exceptions that you have not dealt with. This point may the code be called from other places.

• else: This part of code is always executed if the try code is right and there is no exception, or any errors in the code will not be handled by the try/except block.

• finally: The finally part of code will always executed , even if there is no exception or if there is a problem with the try code.

• In other programming languages you will see something like try and except it, maybe try and catch, or also raise and throw as equivalents.

**Let's create a boot menu, myMenu.py.**

```
#!/user/bin/python3

#myMenu.py

From subprocess import call

FileN ="myMenu.ini"

DES=0

Key_k = 1

CM = 2

Print("Start Menu: ")

Try:

With open(fileN) as f:

myMenuFile = f.readlines()

except IOError:

print("cannot open %s" %(fileN))

for item in myMenuFile

line = item.split(',')

print ("(%s):%s" % (line[KEY_k], line[DES]))

#Get the user input

Run = True
```

```
While(run)

Us_input = input()

#check the input

For item in myMenuFile:

Line = item.spilt(',')

If(us_input == line[KEY_k]):

Print("comm:" + line[CM])

#run the script

Comm = line[CM].rstrip().split()

Print(comm)

Run = false

If len(comm):

Call(comm)

If(run == true):

Print ("your key in not exist in the menu")

Print ("everything is done")
```

Create a menu named menu.ini file that will contain the following:

Start Desk,d, starty

Show ip Address, I, hostname –I

Show cpu speed, s, cat /
sys/devices/system/cpu/cpu0/cpu/cpufreq/scaling_cur_

Freq

Show core temp, t, sudo /opt/vc/bin/vcgencmd measure temp

Exit,x,

● You can add your command and you can customize the list based on your needs..

If you want to execute any other programs from a Python script, you will need to use the command "call". You only wish to use the call part of the subprocess module, so you can simply use the subprocess import call.

● Open the file and read the lines in a menufile array. You can process each item as follows:

Line ['Start', 'Desk','d', 'starty']

You can access each section using the print statement separately, so you can print the key you need to press for a specific command and the description of the command.

Us_input == line[KEY_k]

The call command will require a command and its parameters to be a list, so you will use the split() function to break the command part into a list (every space in the statement will use the function).You should note that after\n is the end of the line character after starty, and this is the end of the line character from mymenu.ini. You will remove the first using the function rstrip() that is used to remove any whitespace.

Start:

Menu:

(d): start Desk

(i): Show ip Address

(s): show cpu speed

(t): show core temp

(y): exit

## Using Python for automation

In this part, you will mainly work with the command line. You will also work with the Raspberry Pi by using a graphical user interface (GUI).

It will be very easy to get the input from the graphical user interface in a natural way. Python supports this. Much like any other programming language, you will use the Tkinter module that provides a lot of good controls and tools to create graphical user interfaces.

The app you will make is to convert the encryption application into a graphical user interface instead of using the command line.

Make sure that you have completed the instructions in the previous part; encryptdecrypt.py program

If you want to use Tkinter (one of add-ons of python), you will need to make sure that it is installed. By default it will be installed on the standard Raspbian image, but let's confirm that by importing it for a Python shell.

>>> import Tkinter

If it doesn't exist you will see an error (import error). In any case, you can install it using the command:

Sudo apt-get install python3-tk

If it did load , you will use the following command to read more:

>> help (tkinter)

Also, you can find a lot of information about the classes, functions and methods by writing the following command:

>>> help(tkinter.Button)

If you want to list any valid commands, you should write the following command in your shell:

>>> dir (tkinter.button)

Now let's use the tkinter to develop a GUI for the encrypt program:

```
#!/usr/bin/python3

#encrypt.py

Import encrypt as ENC

Import tkinter as TK

def encbutton():

encryptVal.set(ENC.encryptText(encryptVal.get(), keyVal.get))

def decButton():

encryptVal.set(ENC.encryptText(encryptVal.get(). –keyVal.get()))
```

```
#Tkinter application

Root =TK.TK()


Root.title("Enc/Dec application")

#control values

encryptVal = TK.StringVar()

enryptVal.set("this is a message")

keyVal = TK.IntVar()

keyVal.set(20)

promp = "Enter your message to encrypt: "

Key_k = "Key: "

Labl_1 = TK.label(root, text = promp, width=len(promp), bg='red' )

texEnter=tk.Entry(root, textvariable =encryptVal, width = len(promp))

encbutton = TK.Button(root, text="enc", command=encbutton)

decButton = TK.Button(root, text="dec", command=decbutton)

labl_2 = TK.label(root, textvariable=keyVal, width=9)

#Layout

Labl_1.grid(row=0, cloumnspan=2, sticky=TK.E + TK.w)

texEnter.grid(row=1, cloumnspan=2, sticky=TK.E+TK.W)

encbutton.grid(row=2, column=0, sticky=TK.E)
```

decbutton.grid(row=2, column=0, sticky=TK.W)

labl_2grid(row=3, column=1, sticky=TK.W)

TK.mainloop() #end of the program

In this program we start by importing modules

First one is the encrypt/decrypt file and the second one is the tkinter module.

The encbutton() and decbutton functions will be run when click on the encrypt and decrypt buttons

Now let's take a look at the code

Labl_1 = TK.label(root, text=promp, width=len(promp), bg='red')

All of the controls have to be linked to the window, you have to determine your tkinter window root. You will set the text using the text variable as shown. You have to set it to a string named promp that we defined previously with the text. You also can set the width to match the number of characters of the message, but it's not necessary to do that. You set the background color by using bg = 'red'.

In the next line of code, you defined the textEntry(root, textvariable=encryptVal, width=len(promp)), you also defined textvariable as a useful way to link variables to the contents of the box that is a string variable. You can access the text using textEnter.get() if you want, but this will allow you to separate the data you got it from the code which handles the graphical user interface. Use a Tkinter StringVar() to access it directly. The encryptVal variable used to update the Entry widget is linked to the .set() command.

Encbutton = TK.button(root, text=t"Encrypt", command=encButton)

decbutton = TK.button(root, text="decrypt", command=encButton)

In this case, you can set a function to call it when the button is pressed:

```
def encbutton():

encryptVal.set(ENC.encryptText(encryptVal.get(), keyVal.get))
```

## Drive the hardware with python

One of the features of the Raspberry Pi is to set it from home computers; it has the ability to interface with any hardware.

The General purpose input – output (GPIO) pins can control a lot of low level electronics from LEDs to motors and displays.

## Controlling an LED in Python

You will need:

• Female to male wire (4)

• Breadboard

• RGB LED

- 470 ohm resistors (3)

This figure show you the difference between the RGB LED and the other LED:

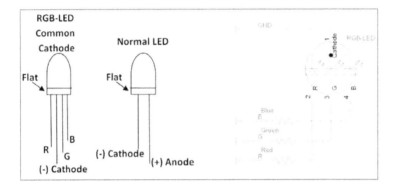

## Controlling an LED in python (wiring)

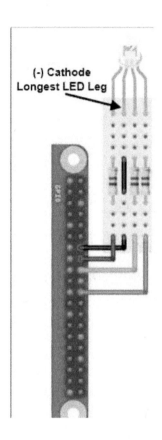

**Controlling an LED in Python (coding)**

#!user/pin/python3

#led.py

```
Import RPi.GPIO as GPIO

import time

#RGB LED

# now setup the hardware

RGB_Ena = 1; RGB_Dis = 0

#LED Configuration

RGB_R = 16; RGB_G = 18; RGB_B=22

RGB = (RGB_R, RGB_G, RGB_B)

Def led_set():

#wiring

GPIO.setmode(GPIO.BOARD)

#ports

For val in RGB:

GPIO.setup(val, GPIO.OUT)

Def main():

Led_set()

For val in RGB:

GPIO.output(val, RGB_Ena)

Print("LED is on now ")

Time.sleep(7)
```

```
GPIO.output(val, RGB_Dis)

Print ("LED is off now ")

Try:

Main()

Finally:

GPIO.cleanup()

Print("Everything is closed now, the END")

#End of the program
```

## Control the LED using a button (wiring)

**You will need:**

- **Female to male wires**

- **Breadboard**

- **Push button switch**

- **General purpose LED**

- **470 ohm resistors (2)**

- **Breadboard wire**

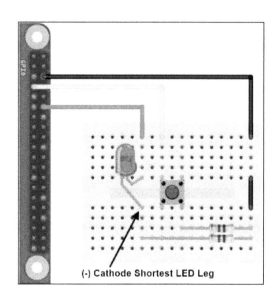

(-) Cathode Shortest LED Leg

## Control the LED using a button (coding)

#!/usr/bin/python3

#control.py

Import time

Import RPi.GPIO as GPIO

Import os

#close the script

debugging = True

nd = True

#setup the hardware

```
#GPIO

#config

MODE = GPIO.BOARD

Sht_BIN = 7

LD = 12

Def gpio_Set():

#wiring

GPIO.semode(GPIO.MODE)

#ports

GPIO.setupt(sht_BIN, GPIO.IN, pull_up_down = GPIO.PUD_UP)

GPIO.Setup(LD,GPIO.OUT)


Def doShut():

If(debugging):print("you pressed the button")

Time.sleep(4)

If GPIO.input(Sht_BIN):

If(debugging):print("skip the shutdown (<4sec)")

else:

if(debugging):print("do you want to shut down the RPi NOW")

GPIO.output(LD,0)
```

```
Time.sleep(0.6)

GPIO.output(LD, 1)

If(ND):os.system("flite –tWarning 3 2 1' ")

If (debugging == false):os.system("sudo shutdown h now")

If(debugging):GPIO.cleanup()

If(debugging):exit()


def main():

GPIO_set()

GPIO.output(LD, 1)

While True:

If(debugging):print("you can press the button")

If GPIO.input(sht_BTN)==False:

doShut()

time.sleep(2)

try:

main()

finally:

GPIO.cleanup()

print("every ting is closed now. The End")
```

#End of the program

## Questions for Chapter 8

1.  Using Python, create a file and put your name and your friends names into that file.

2.  Design and develop an LED blinking system using a button and 3 LEDs.

3.  Make the three LEDs blink in sequence order.

4.  Design a graphical user interface to control the system in Question 3.

# Chapter 9

# Final Project

**What you will learn in this chapter:**

Build a media center using the Raspberry Pi

**What you will need for this chapter:**

Raspberry Pi board

4 GB SD card or micro SD

HDMI cable

Ethernet cable

In this chapter you will build a media center on the Raspberry Pi board.

The first thing you will do is choose an operating system. I mean the appropriate operating system for the project because you will focus on making the Pi into a media center. There are two operating systems for this purpose; the first one is OpenELEC (Open Embedded Linux Entertainment Center), and the second one is OSMC(Open Source Media Center). In this project you will use the OSMC , so let's do the following:

● Download the OS.

● Install the OS on the SD card.


## Download and Install the OSMC

Now you should choose the correct version of OSMC so you can download and install it. You can go to RaspberryPi.org, this is the official website for the Raspberry PI. As shown before in the past chapters, you can use this web site as a support community for you because you can share your experience the other Raspberry Pi users or read about theirs.

Now go to the main page and then choose DOWNLOADS. There, you will find a list of all the options of the operating systems you can choose from, or you can start working with Noobs that provide a look at what the Raspberry PI can do. You will find under these lists a third party operating system, and at this part you will find the OSMC, so just click on it.

● After completing the download, you can now install it. Make sure that you have the appropriate SD card that you can use on the

Raspberry Pi. If you don't have WinRAR, just go to the WinRAR website and install it and extract the image.

Now it's time to burn the operating system onto the SD card. Make sure that the file is ended with .img, then open the image burning program and burn it.

After burning the image on the SD card, you can set up everything now. You will need the following hardware:

## The power supply

This power supply will make the difference to the Raspberry Pi, because if the pi is underpowered it will tell you it doesn't enough power during high-CPU usage.

## Video – Audio Output

You can use the HDMI cable to connect your Raspberry Pi, but you should keep two things in mind: the length and the stiffness of the cable.

## Internet Cable (Ethernet Cable)

You use this cable to connect you device to the Internet, but you can also use the USB Wi-Fi dongle.

Now it's time to plug everything in:

- Plug the Raspberry Pi to the power supply and USB devices.

- Plug your preferred video/audio cable to either the HDMI or RCA ports.

- Hook the Raspberry Pi to the TV.


## Start working with the OSMC

- This operating system uses a front end called Kodi. In this part you are going to become very familiar with the OSMC (Operating System Media Center), and you are going to do the following:

- Work and navigate the keyboard

- Start looking at the settings

- Set up and configure the network


## Work and navigate with the keyboard

If you use your PC or your laptop, you may do most of your actions using the mouse to click on different menus or to open programs.

You mainly use your keyboard only when you enter your IP Address, typing something like an email, or playing a game. On the OSMC you can navigate with your mouse, but it will be much better than your keyboard and that depends on the version of your Raspberry Pi board.

The home screen of the OSMC:

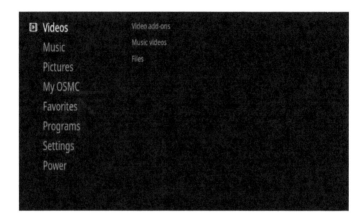

OSMC has a lot of different ways that you can use the content. I will show you how to stream it from different sources.

The Files menu is where videos can be found. We will discover how to get videos into the right place so you can watch them later. The most important thing you should know is the video add-ons. This is where Kodi comes in, and you will spend a lot of time adding new programs and watching your favorite videos.

**Music**

This screen is like the video screen. You can store your sounds or audio files if you open it from this screen. Like with videos , if you stored a collection of audio files somewhere, you can access it from the

OSMC from this screen as well. Also, you will find the music add-ons like the video add-ons.

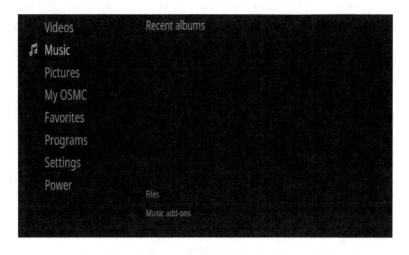

## The settings

## In the settings, you can find the following info

● File manager: If you want to transfer something from a USB onto the Raspberry Pi like pictures or movies, you will open the directory from the file manager.

● System info: This will give an overview of the things running on the Raspberry Pi, and it also provides you with information like the IP address, summary, storage, memory, and so on.

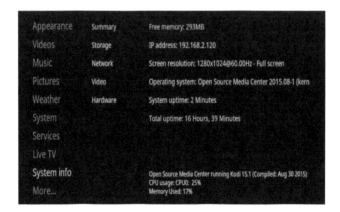

● Profiles: The profiles are something like the users on the Windows operating system; you add users, delete, and edit something like the privileges similar to any operating system.

MyOSMC

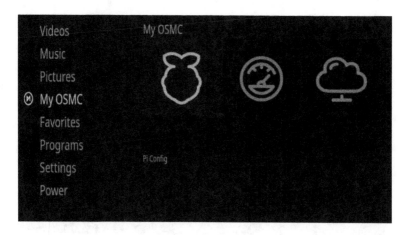

This screen handles hardware, overclocking, networking, and controls to connect the OSMC from another computer in case you want to transfer the file.

Wi-Fi

If you want to connect to the Internet wirelessly, you will use the Wi-Fi.

And you can set up it from this screen as shown:

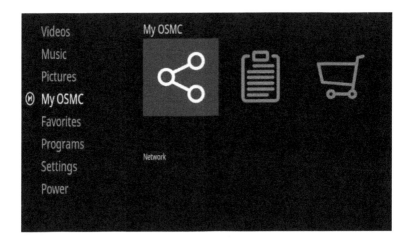

After plugging your Wi-Fi dongle and running your OSMC, you can go to the network and then click "Wireless." Click yes and finally apply.

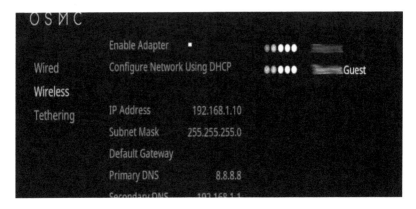

## Install video add—ons

If you want to install new applications on the OSMC, you will navigate over to videos: Add-ons and press enter. Any apps(add-ons) that have been installed will be found here.

Toonjet

TwitchTV

USTVnow

YouTube

Get more...

There are many choices you can choose from. You will scroll a long list of choices and take time to choose one. You can install it easily by dimming anything and then pressing enter, but you should look at the language of the app because the same app may have multilingual versions and you may prefer a specific one.

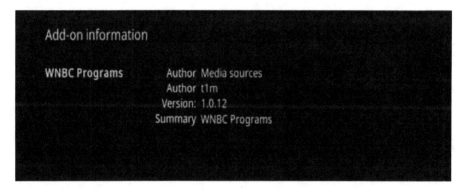

Add-on information

WNBC Programs          Author  Media sources
                       Author  t1m
                       Version: 1.0.12
                       Summary  WNBC Programs

After installing a few apps , press backspace to see what apps you have installed.

## Music add-ons

If you interested in music you can also do the same thing. There are a lot of streaming options available that you can add on the Raspberry Pi. You can go to music by using the keyboard and pressing enter on music.

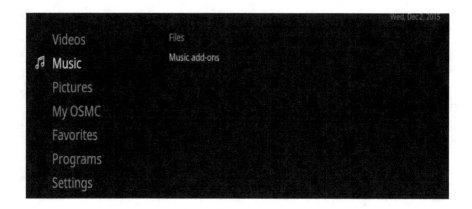

## Move and copy your files

You will use now the file manager to copy or move files. From the main page, go to "settings" and then choose "file manager."

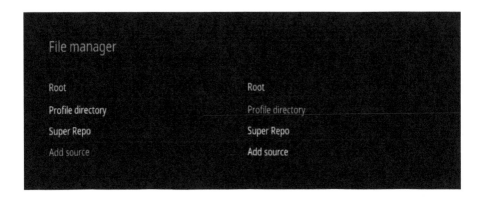

● In this figure you can see that there is a directory called Super Repo. If you plugged in your USB, you can see the directory listed on the file manager screen.

● After inserting your USB stick, scroll to your USB until you see your files and then copy any file you want. For example, llc.mp3, then go to any directory you want and paste it there.

●If you want to play the DVDs and ISOs , the Raspberry Pi can do that but you will need to do the following:

Get the codec, go back to www.raspberrypi.org

- Click on "shop" until you reach to the Raspberry Pi Swag Store and press on that. There are many categories like buy a Pi, Codecs, and so on.

- You will use codec/OS, so choose this.

- For DVDs, you will need an **MPEG-2 LICENSE KEY,** so you will purchase the codec and then press on the license "please click here to buy your mpeg-2 license key."

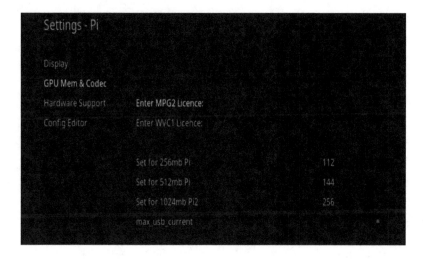

Go to MyOSMC from the main menu, then pi config, and finally to GPU Mem & Codec.

• Keep in mind that not all of the Raspberry Pi boards will process this code.

• If you want to play a DVD you will need to add an external DVD reader to the Raspberry Pi that you connect via USB to your computer.

## Networking

• In this part you will learn how to connect your OSMC over the network.

• You should connect with computers in your home network.

• Everything you will do with your home network can be done with larger networks.

• Some of the benefits of connecting your OSMC is to watch your movies on TV, for example.

• You will focus on your home network instead of Raspberry Pi and OSMC.

## Sharing in Windows

• You should remember how to share with Windows, Samba, and SMB.

• Sharing is one of the easiest things that you can do in Windows. After installing Windows , if you want to share a folder you can just click on it, choose "properties," and then click sharing.

## Sharing in Linux

• If you are using the Linux operating system, you can use SSH (secure shell).

If you want to share your Linux computer and the OSMC, simply do the following:

Open the terminal window and then write this command:

Sudo systememct1 enable sshd

If your computer didn't process this command, don't worry.

You can try the other command:

Sudo service ssh start

And then write the following:

Sudo systememct1 start sshd

## NFS (Network File Share)

- Network file sharing on Linux is something like the sharing in Windows..

- When you want to connect to a remote folder, your computer will be like a local folder.

- It will be more complex to setup the Network File Share than an SSH.

Because you will make the other users someone other than yourself , so you will need to set the permissions.

Sudo mkdir any name / nfs

Sudo shown user: user /nfs

Chmod 777 /nfs

Sudo nano /etc/exports

/nfs    *(rw)

## Samba

This is the last option to share media from your Linux computer to OSMC, and it is Samba.

Now open the terminal window and write the following command:

Sudo nano / etc/samba/smb.conf

We can scroll down all the way and then add our information for the folder we are sharing.

[sharing name]

Path = /samba

Writable = yes

Guest ok = yes

Hosts allow = 192.168.

We can enable and start the Samba service.

Sudo systemct1 enable/start smb

Service smbd start

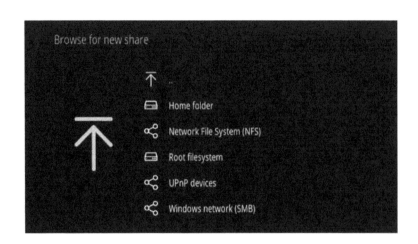

www.ingramcontent.com/pod-product-compliance
Lightning Source LLC
LaVergne TN
LVHW022323060326
832902LV00020B/3626